PRACTICAL PSYCHOLOGY OF LEADERSHIP FOR CRIMINAL JUSTICE OFFICERS

PRACTICAL PSYCHOLOGY OF LEADERSHIP FOR CRIMINAL JUSTICE OFFICERS
A Basic Programmed Text

By

ROBERT J. WICKS

Prison Health Services
Health Services Administration
City of New York, New York
Formerly, Lecturer
Law Enforcement Division
Department of Community Colleges
State of North Carolina

and

ERNEST H. JOSEPHS, JR.

Learning Center Coordinator
Coastal Carolina Community College
Jacksonville, North Carolina

CHARLES C THOMAS • PUBLISHER
Springfield • Illinois • U.S.A.

Published and Distributed Throughout the World by
CHARLES C THOMAS • PUBLISHER
BANNERSTONE HOUSE
301-327 East Lawrence Avenue, Springfield, Illinois, U.S.A.

This book is protected by copyright. No part of it may be reproduced in any manner without written permission from the publisher.

© 1973, by CHARLES C THOMAS • PUBLISHER
ISBN 0-398-02783-8
Library of Congress Catalog Card Number: 72-11621

With THOMAS BOOKS *careful attention is given to all details of manufacturing and design. It is the Publisher's desire to present books that are satisfactory as to their physical qualities and artistic possibilities and appropriate for their particular use.* THOMAS BOOKS *will be true to those laws of quality that assure a good name and good will.*

Printed in the United States of America
W-2

For Our Parents
Mae and Joseph Wicks
&
Grace and Ernest Josephs, Sr.

TO THE STUDENT

YOU ARE ABOUT to be introduced to a textbook quite different from the traditional kind. It is called a PROGRAMMED TEXTBOOK. If you follow the instructions contained herein, you should find this new learning experience to be very gratifying and rewarding.

Your programmed textbook contains the same kind of material that you would expect to find in an ordinary text. The material, however, has been broken down into small, numbered statements or frames. These frames are arranged in a logical, step-by-step pattern, beginning with the more simple concepts and gradually progressing to the more complex ones.

Each frame will teach you a certain amount of information and then will allow you to fill in the blanks that are provided with information that you have just learned. You may write your answers in the blanks provided in the book or on a separate sheet of paper. The important thing here is that you do WRITE DOWN your answers. Before attempting to write your responses, however, you should read the ENTIRE frame. Then after you have written down your answer, you may compare it with the correct response appearing in the right hand column, directly across from each frame. A correct response will send you on to the next frame. If your response is incorrect, you should reread and study the frame until you have mastered it. It is important that you understand each principle before continuing on.

A word of caution: you should at no time look at the responses that appear in the textbook before you have arrived at your own response. An answer shield has been provided in the back of this textbook for your convenience. Therefore, before beginning the first chapter go to the rear of this book and remove the section of paper marked ANSWER SHIELD by tearing it out along the perforated line. You are to use the answer shield by covering the answer column with it before starting to read any of the frames. And as you finish each frame you should slide the answer shield down the page to reveal each book response.

Your programmed textbook is designed to allow you to work at your own rate of speed. As you work through the program you will find that important facts are constantly reviewed to ensure that you remember them.

When you are ready to begin, turn to frame #1, cover the answer column with your answer shield and commence working. Chapter 1 has been made somewhat basic so you can familiarize yourself with this type of text before going on to the more detailed material.

ROBERT J. WICKS
ERNEST H. JOSEPHS, JR.

CONTENTS

	Page
To the Student	vii

Chapter
1. INTRODUCTION 3
2. LEADERSHIP TRAITS 13
3. GUIDELINES OF LEADERSHIP 40
4. LEADERSHIP AND SUPERVISION 66
5. PROBLEM SOLVING 90
6. A REVIEW 100

PRACTICAL PSYCHOLOGY OF LEADERSHIP FOR CRIMINAL JUSTICE OFFICERS

1 INTRODUCTION

The introduction to this text serves the following three-fold purpose:

   1. *To acquaint the reader with various approaches in defining leadership.*
   2. *To acquaint the reader with the objectives of this text.*
   3. *To give the reader a brief exposure to programmed learning.*

1. People will generally agree that good LEADERSHIP must be demonstrated by those in high position, such as the persons who fill the offices of president, governor, and mayor.	(No response required.)
2. Yet, there are numerous other positions in government and private enterprise that require an ability to l-_____ others. Of these positions, the individual involved in law enforcement and correctional work must certainly be included.	lead
3. Law enforcement and correctional personnel are called upon to demonstrate their l-_____ abilities on almost a daily basis.	leadership

4. For example, a _____ (doctor/police officer) is usually the first to arrive at the scene of an accident where people are injured, confused, or otherwise acting irrationally.	police officer
5. When a crowd begins to form in the dining area of a prison, it is understandable that a social scientist _____ (would/would not) be the first to be notified in order to analyze the situation so a course of action might be formulated to prevent a riot.	would not
6. In the above situation, the correction officer, captain, or deputy warden would usually be the first man called so his _____ abilities could be put to the task of restoring order.	leadership
7. In a town where any type of crisis has quickly flared-up, it is not the mayor or local elected official who would first be requested to attend to the problem—there would be no time for that! Once again, the law enforcement officer must quickly demonstrate his capability to _____ others if the disturbance is to be quelled and order restored.	lead

8. There is no doubt then that correction and law enforcement officers are often called upon to be _____ in many difficult situations.	leaders
9. This being the case, it is beneficial to the community and the department if the officers are able to demonstrate a high degree of _____ ability.	leadership
10. But what if the officer does not seem to be a good leader? Can leadership be LEARNED? This is a much disputed question today; one to which there seems to be no clear cut answer.	(No response required.)
11. Despite the controversy over this problem, leadership _____ (is/is not) being taught quite successfully today in the armed forces and in business workshops.	is
12. In these settings, theoretical principles are laid down and then hypothetical situations are created to determine the trainee's ability to apply what he has _____.	learned

13. By making mistakes, by observing how he did or did not employ the basics given to him by the instructor, the trainee gains experience in _____.	leadership
14. The success the military and business have had in teaching BASICS IN LEADERSHIP will be capitalized on in this text. Illustrative law enforcement and correction situations will be provided, and the students will be given typical solutions that have been proved to be effective.	(No response required.)
15. However, to give basics in _____, the approach which will be used to operationally define the concept of leadership must first be decided. There are at least five basic ways that leadership can be viewed.	leadership
16. Leadership can be discussed in terms of POWER. The leader is seen as an individual who has the _____ to change the course of a nation, a state, or a town.	power

17. In the case of an officer of the law, there is enough _____ in his hands to change the course of an event or a person.	power
18. In addition, how a law enforcement officer uses his _____ is important, for it is easily abused by someone in authority.	power
19. Although the amount of power vested in the officer and the way it is used is important, the concept of power is not comprehensive enough to be the only consideration in a discussion of good leadership ability. Thus, examining leadership only in terms of _____ is too limited.	power
20. Leadership can also be viewed as a FUNCTION OF MANAGEMENT. In other words, the good leader is one who can ensure that the goals of the group are achieved.	(No response required.)
21. Although the assurance that the common good of the group is met is vital, leadership being defined solely as a function of _____ is still too limited.	management

22. Leadership can also be studied in terms of SOCIAL ACCEPTABILITY. For example, voters often detect certain likable characteristics in a political candidate that sway them to his side. If we allow these reasons to serve as the basis of choice, we are defining leadership in terms of social _____.	acceptability
23. However, poor leaders are often chosen for incorrect reasons such as physical appearance and the promise of favors, so s-_____ a-_____ is inadequate as the only measure of leadership ability.	social acceptability
24. Thus, it _____ (would/would not) be feasible to use social acceptability as the sole criterion for effective leadership.	would not
25. Still another approach to leadership comes about through the ANALYSIS of LEADERSHIP BEHAVIOR. By establishing some pattern of standard behavior from the study of actions, mannerisms, etc., of successful leaders, we would be setting guidelines through the analysis of _____ _____.	leadership behavior

26. However, most successful leaders did not demonstrate any standardized behavioral activities. Though it is close to the method to be used in this text, we might conclude that the method of analyzing leadership behavior ——————— (is/is not) somewhat lacking in scope. | is

27. Thus, we have now determined that there are several aspects that may warrant some consideration in establishing abilities for leadership. But when considered apart, each one proves to be ———————. | limited, inadequate, etc.

28. The approaches that we have just discussed in an attempt to operationally define leadership are:
   (1) ———————.
   (2) function of m———————.
   (3) social a———————.
   (4) analysis of ——————— ———————. | power
management
acceptability
leadership/ behavior

29. Again, the four approaches that have shown to be inadequate in defining leadership are:

(1) ———————.
(2) ——————— of ———————.
(3) ——————— ———————.
(4) ——————— of ——————— ———————.

power
function/
management
social/
acceptability
analysis/
leadership/
behavior

---

30. The only approach that seems left, and the one used in this book is called the TRAIT approach. In this text a number of core traits and LEADERSHIP GUIDELINES are presented for consideration by the officer.

(No response required.)

---

31. It must be admitted, however, that, as in the case of the other approaches, the trait method also is lacking in some respects.

(No response required.)

---

32. Since the list of traits which could aid in the development of ——————— is almost inexhaustible, some traits had to be sacrificed for the sake of brevity.

leadership

33. The same can be said for the ―――― guidelines included in this text, as these too are illimitable. Furthermore, it does not necessarily follow that once an officer finishes this book, he will be qualified as a good leader. This, obviously, would be too presumptuous.	leadership
34. However, with the tr-―――― approach, the officer can be exposed to a number of basic factors which should, along with the g-――――, give him a number of characteristics that can be easily understood and employed.	trait guidelines
35. Also, when applied in the illustrative situations provided, the traits and guidelines should assist the officer better than any other approach to date in attempting to deal EFFECTIVELY with actual problems in the field.	(No response required.)

36. Moreover, in the latter part of this text, a chapter is devoted entirely to the step-by-step way in which a person should approach most problems in order to handle them _____. This chapter will demonstrate to the officer a method which is organized so that the task is handled in such a way as to decrease the chances of missing any of the elements involved.	effectively
37. And so, this text, if studied carefully, should aid the officer in understanding how to deal with a problem systematically. In addition, it should provide enough traits, guidelines, and illustrative law enforcement/correction examples to enable the officer to approach his daily duties equipped with the tools necessary to increase his proficiency.	(No response required.)

2 LEADERSHIP TRAITS

Upon completion of this chapter, the student should be able to perform the following objectives:

1. *Illustrate the process through which one's leadership abilities can be improved.*
2. *Explain numerous leadership traits that will be helpful in generally improving duty performance.*

1. As the title infers, this chapter is concerned with _____ traits. Here, a number of traits will be presented which should assist the officer in developing his LEADERSHIP potential.	leadership
2. The authors feel that the study and discussion of leadership traits is the most effective way of improving one's _____ potential.	leadership
3. It should be noted, however, that the study of leadership traits alone will not provide a *Golden Key* to becoming a good leader. Leadership, then is more than a combination of particular _____.	traits

4. Rather, leadership is the ability to effectively direct a group of individuals to accomplish or put forth optimal effort to achieve a goal or goals on a continuing basis.	(No response required.)
5. By successfully encouraging subordinates to demonstrate professionalism in the accomplishment of tasks assigned to them, one is demonstrating _____ ability.	leadership
6. Thus, the proper direction of subordinates to accomplish assigned tasks in an efficient and versed manner requires an ability to _____ others.	lead
7. The essence of leadership consists, then, of two basic criteria. They are (1) _____ (t) _____ and the development of GUIDELINES in employing these traits.	leadership traits
8. If this point is understood, the controversy over whether leadership can or cannot be learned is _____ (affected/avoided).	avoided

9. This text is based on the assumption that the best way to aid a person—a law enforcement/correction officer—to become a better leader is to give him a number of _____ and (g)_____ to use. (The guidelines will be further discussed in Chapter 3: "Guidelines of Leadership.")	traits guidelines
10. As was noted in Chapter 1, leadership is being successfully taught in the military and in _____ workshops.	business
11. Therefore, it is possible to offer a person of average ability a number of **TOOLS** and reasonably expect him to improve his leadership techniques. Leadership traits, then, are the _____ of a good leader.	tools
12. However, despite the success of this method, it is not foolproof. In other words, it _____ (promises/does not promise) the student that he will become a good leader. Such as assumption _____ (would/would not) be presumptuous.	does not promise would

13. It does, however, promise the student that the tools to be presented should aid him in the exercise and development of his ———— abilities if he takes them into account.	leadership
14. Let's look now at the first trait to be discussed which is DEPENDABILITY. The officer who is trusted by his superiors, peers, and subordinates is considered to be ————.	dependable
15. The officer who is punctual, who does not make excuses for mistakes, and who puts forth maximum effort on a *continuing* basis is a ———— one.	dependable
16. In other words, the officer who is dependable is one who can be ————(ally) counted on by the staff with whom he works.	continually
17. Superiors, subordinates, and peers realize that they can count on the dependable officer for ————(al) support.	continual

18. On the other hand, an officer who is often late for work, who has a high rate of absenteeism, and who has difficulty working with his fellow officers cannot be _____ upon to effectively carry out a task.	depended
19. It should be noted here, that the ability of a subordinate to effectively carry out a task reflects the _____ abilities of his superior.	leadership

20. Accordingly, difficulties in interpersonal relations, perennial tardiness, and a high rate of absenteeism by an officer should prompt the superior to: (choose one)
  a. Have him fired before his co-workers pick-up his habits.
  b. Find out what problems the officer is having that may result in his being undependable.
  c. Suspend him from the force until he realizes his mistakes.
	b.

21. A good leader then is always ALERT to the early signs shown by a subordinate who is having (pr)_____.	problems

22. Often, difficulties can be worked out when they are in the early stages of development if the superior is ———— to any indications of troubled subordinates.	alert
23. However, if the superior ignores problems as they begin to develop among his subordinates, the problems might: (choose one) a. Work themselves out, thereby reducing tensions that may have been created had the superior intervened. b. Get completely out of hand and resistant to any subsequent efforts made by the superior to correct them.	b.
24. And so, upon discovering that a subordinate is having problems similar to those mentioned previously because he is exhausted from working an extra job, for example, the following course of action should be taken: (choose one) a. Convince him to give up the part time job before he becomes financially dependent upon it. b. Tell him that *moonlighting* will not be tolerated in any form. c. Suspend him from duty as an example to others who may be contemplating getting an extra job.	a.

25. The point being made then is that a subordinate should be counselled in the beginning before his problem gets ———— of ————.	out/hand
26. Handling a problem promptly, indeed may prevent a potentially good officer from becoming an (un)———— one.	undependable
27. Remember, a ———— officer is one who is TRUSTED by the other members of the staff or department.	dependable
28. The task of the dependable officer, therefore, becomes much easier to perform because his subordinates, peers, and superiors have confidence in him. In other words, they ———— him.	trust
29. A second leadership trait that will enable the officer to build confidence in himself and increase the respect of his fellow officers is good JUDGMENT.	(No response required.)

30. The quality of being able to SURVEY all possible ALTERNATIVES before making a decision is called good _____.	judgment
31. Law enforcement and correction officers come into contact with many volatile situations which require that a decision be made. Such a decision should be based upon good, sound _____.	judgment
32. Judgment, then, is the ability to be able to _____ all possible _____ before reaching a decision.	survey/ alternatives
33. A decision, for example, on what steps to take during the initial stage of a riot, or what to do first at the scene of a terrible accident requires that the officer exercise good _____.	judgment
34. When a situation such as the above occurs, the officer must be able to weigh the facts and determine a logical course of action based on what he knows. He must, therefore, prevent EMOTION and fear from affecting his _____.	judgment

35. If the officer in the previous illustration allows himself to become ———(al) or fearful, he will be unable to logically appraise the situation in order to make a wise judgment.	emotional
36. Spur of the moment decisions, made in the heat of emotion, are often wrong. Thus, emotion must be (el)——— from the decision making process.	eliminated
37. In addition to making a sound judgment, a third leadership trait, KNOWLEDGE, must be present as well.	(No response required.)
38. Knowledge is more than simply knowing the rules and regulations. Most officers know them well. The successful leader must also stay abreast of technical—professional literature in the field and take time out to become familiar with the men under him before he can consider his overall ——— of the job as being sufficient.	knowledge

39. If, for example, an officer believes that his superior knows him and the problems he has on the job, the officer will have greater confidence in him as a _____.	leader
40. Thus, the leader must read as much (1)_____ as possible in his field and always be open to the (p)_____ of his subordinates if he is to be considered _____ (able).	literature problems knowledgeable
41. The next, and fourth, leadership trait to be considered is INITIATIVE. Progress and change would rarely take place in any field if its leaders did not possess _____.	initiative
42. As one might expect, initiative is a rarely demonstrated trait. The reason is quite simple. People are afraid they will make a mistake if they try something new on their own _____.	initiative
43. Accordingly, the individual who often finds himself *out on a limb* may well be the one who isn't afraid to show _____.	initiative

Leadership Traits

44. Although it can get pretty lonely *out on that limb,* the leader who is not willing to take the _____ when the circumstances demand it will never be exceptional.	initiative
45. Initiative then, like knowledge, must be DEVELOPED. It is not an innate (with us from birth) characteristic. And since initiative *is* a trait that must be _____ let's determine how one might go about doing so.	developed

46. To begin, select from the list below those characteristics that you feel can be considered elements of a leader's initiative.
    a. Just follow instructions to the letter.
    b. Seek responsibility.
    c. Shows alertness.
    d. Endeavors to utilize available resources.
	
	b.
	c.
	d.

47. Let's take a moment to develop the selections in the previous frame. For example, the officer who is content to just take orders and not be held accountable for anything apparently does not seek _____.	responsibility

48. The officer who possesses an awareness of his duties, responsibilities, and the course of events that develop around him is said to be _____.	alert
49. The officer who strives to use all of the tools available to him and can improve when necessary, not taking the time to excuse himself from completing a task for lack of material or men when the job can be accomplished without such aids, is said to be one who fully utilizes the _____ to which he has access.	resources
50. Thus, responsibility, alertness, and the utilization of available resources are all elements of the leadership trait called _____.	initiative
51. Before continuing on, let's take a moment to reexamine the four leadership traits that we have discussed.	(No response required.)
52. First, the leader who develops the trust and confidence of his subordinates possesses the trait of (d)_____.	dependability

53. Secondly, the officer who has the ability to logically survey all possible alternatives before making a decision possesses the leadership trait of good (j)_____.	judgment
54. Thirdly, the leader who constantly strives to stay abreast of his field by reading and who makes himself aware of his subordinate's problems is (k) _____ in his field.	knowledgeable
55. And fourthly, an officer who seeks responsibility and who demonstrates alertness and resourcefulness in the accomplishment of his job has developed the leadership trait called (i)_____.	initiative

56. Without referring to previous frames, list the four leadership traits that you have learned.
    a. _____.
    b. _____.
    c. _____.
    d. _____.
	dependability
	judgment
	knowledge
	initiative

57. Now to continue on, a fifth, and very important leadership trait to be developed is INTEGRITY. Since the peace officer deals with a criminal population on a daily basis, the potential for corruption is great; therefore, it is essential that the officer maintain _____ in the performance of his duty.	integrity
58. On the opposite side of the *coin* from integrity lies dishonesty, and the leader must always be alert for signs indicating *dishonesty*. In a prison setting, for example, the presence of contraband or the show of favor toward certain prisoners may indicate _____ on the part of some officer(s).	dishonesty
59. In a police precinct, the presence of an *unwritten policy* which forbids the giving of a violation for a particular offense to a certain party constitutes _____.	dishonesty
60. As an illustration of the above, a patrolman in a large city precinct was once admonished when he said that he was going to *ticket* illegally parked trucks on a street within his jurisdiction. He was soon informed that, if he did, he would be subsequently transferred.	(No response required.)

61. Often, the signs of dishonesty may not be as *concrete* as in the previous illustration. They may only be vaguely noticeable in the types of arrests made. For example, a precinct may have a good record except for the sale of drugs, even though the drug traffic is known to be *high* in the area. A situation such as this may indicate _____ on the part of some officers.	dishonesty
62. The dishonest correction or law enforcement officer, too, is not often someone who can be easily distinguished. Just as the violation that he commits is not always discernable in (con)_____ terms, he too becomes somewhat obscure despite the signs of corruption in a precinct or department.	concrete
63. Most dishonest officers, however, were _____ when they joined the force. Usually they become corrupt over a long period of time.	honest
64. We should, at this point, examine some of the extenuating circumstances, then, that may contribute to the dishonesty of an officer.	(No response required.)

65. On the street, for example, the officer has a certain amount of power, but often does not receive a salary commensurate with the risks he takes or public support for the job he is trying to do. Inadequate salary has long attributed to _____ on the part of an officer.	dishonesty
66. In response to these deficiencies on the job, the officer might slowly come to believe that whatever he can get for himself is *only fair*. An (in)_____ salary, then, may be a contributing factor toward the loss of an officer's (in)_____.	inadequate integrity
67. In making excuses for his dishonest activities, the officer in the previous illustration may be tempted to make further rationalizations for other, more serious, infractions of the law. Rarely does the course of events cease with one _____ act.	dishonest
68. For example, the officer may accept *gifts* to look the other way when some illegal activity like gambling is taking place in the precinct. An officer who would take part in such an enormity has certainly lost his _____.	integrity

69. When the officer allows his integrity to go *down the drain,* it is only a matter of time before his SELF-RESPECT goes too.	(No response required.)
70. Normally an individual who compromises his integrity attempts to prolong the loss of his self-_____ by excusing himself with thoughts like, "A little gambling isn't going to hurt anyone. Besides, they never seem to give me the support that I need, and the money will certainly be helpful. It's not as if I'm really doing anything wrong."	respect
71. Here, the law enforcement officer is masking the truth from himself through such rationalizations. Yet, when he finally comes to terms with himself, and he will, he will have lost his self-respect and, along with it, an essential ingredient to becoming a _____ in the law enforcement field.	leader
72. A law enforcement officer usually becomes corrupt very gradually, until before he realizes it, he has reached the stage of deep involvement in (dis)_____ pursuits.	dishonest

73. In the correction facility, the officer is also subjected to an environment which can cause him to become _____ if he is not careful.	dishonest
74. The prison population contains some of the best MANIPULATORS in society. In order for them to obtain money for drugs or to support themselves without working, they have learned, while on the street, to (m)_____ people with great facility.	manipulate
75. As a case in point, an inmate may observe the officer or civilian employee in the institution for a long period of time before approaching him. During that time, the inmate is looking for WEAKNESSES in the individual.	(No response required.)
76. Upon finding what he feels to be the officer's _____, the inmate will make his move by trying to obtain a small FAVOR.	weakness
77. In such an instance, the inmate may seek a _____ by feigning inferiority and appealing to an officer's possible need to feel important.	favor

78. In order for the correction or law enforcement officer to prevent himself or his men, if he is in a supervisory position, from becoming a slave to dishonest pursuit on the job, he should:

a. Never give in to a dishonest act NO MATTER HOW SMALL IT MAY SEEM. b. Ensure that all reports and statements made are true. c. Deal with prisoners or previous offenders not only humanely, but also with a certain amount of skepticism, being ever aware of their ability as criminals to (m)_____ people.	manipulate
79. The fact that the primary danger to integrity occurs when an officer is tempted to make a seemingly _____ (large/small) concession to a dishonest interest cannot be overemphasized.	small
80. It is with such an apparently innocent act that gross violations of honest justice begin.	(No response required.)

81. Now let's focus our attention on the sixth leadership trait which, though less important than integrity, is still an essential characteristic of leadership. It is called TACT. The officer who makes a successful effort to communicate with others without offending them possess —————.	tact
82. Of all the attributes covered thus far, tact is probably the most elusive of all. Disappointingly enough, many would-be leaders feel that dealing with people without offending them is unimportant. This is, of course, far from the truth.	(No response required.)
83. One might conclude, then, from the foregoing that RESPECT and ————— go hand-in-hand. A show of concern for other individuals in the way one deals with them can indicate to a leader's subordinates and superiors that he thinks enough of them to treat them (re)—————(ly).	tact respectfully

84. Thus, tact is the show of _____ for _____. Once other personnel feel that an officer will go out of his way to be considerate, they will want to work with him even more.	respect others
85. And so, when a superior has to correct an officer who has erred in his duty, _____ becomes a particularly important trait to have. 86. In correcting the officer, the superior should make him realize that his behavior was incorrect and possibly irresponsible without alienating him. This can be done by concentrating on the details of the mistake and how it can be avoided without degrading the individual himself. In other words, the superior should show _____ for his subordinates.	tact respect
87. Furthermore, when seeking to find who is at fault for a wrongdoing, the superior should make it clear that the primary reason he is following up the error is to determine WHY it was done. Once the superior determines _____ the error was committed, the officer in question can then be taught how his judgment proved to be incorrect.	why

88. Thus, when it becomes necessary for a superior to correct a mistake made by a subordinate, it would behoove him to focus his attention on the ─────── and not on the ───────.	mistake/ subordinate
89. Let's now consider a seventh leadership trait which merits some attention in the section. This trait encompassing a list of synonymous terms such as impartiality, fairness, reasonableness, and uprightness is called JUSTICE.	(No response required.)
90. In instances where a department has a biased commander who demonstrates favoritism in his assignments, recommendations for promotions, and punishments, the value of ─────── is especially obvious.	justice
91. In a unit such as the above, morale is low and teamwork non-existent. Instead, there are small cliques of individuals who are either in the leader's favor or his ire. One can then plainly see how (in)─────── to subordinates can render a unit ineffective.	injustice

92. When intra-rivalry infiltrates a department, it leads to such dissension that the department will never be able to function at an acceptable level.	(No response required.)
93. Therefore, it is essential for an officer to be fair with his men, constantly on the guard against prejudice, and never in the habit of holding grudges against certain members of the force. The leader, then, must practice _____ in his relationships with subordinates.	justice
94. Furthermore, the officer must always be aware that disciplinary action for a minor offense, such as continual tardiness, would be (un)_____ if he had not previously given the offender a verbal warning and taken time to counsel with him.	unjust
95. If an officer feels that he has been warned and assisted with a problem, he and his fellow officers will probably not view his punishment as _____ if he continually commits the same minor infraction.	unjust

96. Therefore, disciplinary action is _____ for habitual minor offenses only after the superior has tried all in his power to bring the difficulty to the person's attention.	just
97. To continue on the eighth and final leadership trait to be discussed in this chapter is BEARING. Like tact, this characteristic is not easily pinned down, thus making it hard to define.	(No response required.)
98. However, an officer who carries himself and conducts his daily activities in a manner becoming a defender of justice—to the point where he inspires confidence—is said to have _____.	bearing
99. If anything, bearing makes the officer's job (e)_____, because those who observe his poise credit him with self-confidence and are encouraged to serve with him, under him, and as his superior officers.	easier

100. If the superior can conduct himself in a dignified manner, he will, indeed, find that the aura created by the impression he gives will truly make his commands more acceptable to those serving under him.	(No response required.)
101. The eight traits designed to provide a good foundation upon which to build effective leadership qualities have now been presented. But, before concluding this section, these traits with which we have been working should be reviewed.	(No response required.)
102. To begin, the officer who can always be counted on to give continual support to his subordinates, to be punctual, and who always gives his *all* to his work possesses the leadership trait called ————.	dependability
103. A law enforcement or correction officer who carefully *weighs* and logically surveys all possible alternatives before making a decision is demonstrating good ————.	judgment

104. Emotion _____ (is/is not) an element of judgment.	is not
105. Dependability inspires (tr)_____ on the part of fellow officers.	trust
106. The officer who knows his job, his men, and stays abreast of new advancements in the field is said to be _____.	knowledgeable
107. Taking calculated risks when necessary and being willing to try out new ideas demonstrates _____.	initiative
108. An essential requirement of any good leader is that he be above reproach in his treatment of both criminals and subordinates. In other words, he must not lose his _____.	integrity
109. Honesty is synonymous with _____.	integrity
110. The corrupt law enforcement or correction officer usually becomes this way very _____.	gradually

111. The leader who can correct a subordinate without offending him personally possesses _____.	tact
112. The officer who treats all of his subordinates fairly and shows no favoritism is applying the leadership trait, _____.	justice
113. Dignity and poise describe the final leadership trait discussed in this chapter. It is _____.	bearing
114. Please list the eight leadership traits that you have now learned in the following blank spaces: a. _____. b. _____. c. _____. d. _____. e. _____. f. _____. g. _____.	 dependability judgment knowledge initiative justice integrity bearing
115. We might conclude by noting simply that a conscientious effort to develop and master the leadership traits covered in this chapter can result in the officer becoming a better leader. It depends only on how much effort he wants to expend in this area.	(No response required.)

3 GUIDELINES OF LEADERSHIP

Upon completion of this chapter, the student should be able to perform the following objectives:
1. Explain the four guidelines that can be helpful in developing leadership abilities.
2. Explain and practice the procedure for the full implementation and utilization of the leadership guidelines.

1. As one might infer from the title of this chapter, there are, in addition to the leadership traits previously discussed, several ──────── of leadership which will help the law enforcement or correction officer to become a more proficient leader.	guidelines
2. These guidelines are principles which are outgrowths of the leadership traits. Therefore, one might expect to find some OVERLAP between the leadership traits and ────────.	guidelines
3. However, despite some ────────(ing), the guidelines are worthy enough to warrant separate treatment here.	overlapping

Guidelines of Leadership

4. As we explore these guidelines, the reader will find that they provide added tools for use in the further development of his leadership abilities.	(No response required.)
5. Of the four guidelines to be discussed, the first to receive attention—and probably the most important—is the CONSTRUCTIVE USE OF AUTHORITY.	(No response required.)
6. This guideline presupposes that, unless subordinates are taught to show mature judgment and ultimately seek to utilize this ability, the supervisory officer will fail as a leader while trying to do everything himself. Thus, the leader must encourage subordinates to _____ their _____ _____.	use/authority constructively
7. The leader must remember that he is placed in command to utilize the individuals assigned to him, not to do their work for them. In other words, he must learn to DELEGATE his _____ to subordinates.	authority

8. If an officer in a supervisory position is unable or unwilling to _____ authority, he will never succeed as a leader.	delegate
9. How, then might the law enforcement or correction officer encourage his subordinates to utilize authority constructively?	(No response required.)
10. The officer can begin by demonstrating a WILLINGNESS to assume RESPONSIBILITY from his superiors. By displaying his _____ to accept _____ himself, the leader will be setting an example for his men to follow.	willingness responsibility
11. Unless the leader is _____ to take on duties assigned to him, and unless he accepts the _____ for the execution of these duties, he will experience considerable difficulty in encouraging his subordinates to do so.	willing responsibility
12. In addition to accepting responsibility, the leader may further encourage his men by providing as many and varied OPPORTUNITIES as possible to involve them in tasks of an advanced nature.	(No response required.)

13. For example, the officer assigned to a *beat* may, from time to time, be given a chance to ride patrol or work with the desk sergeant. Here, the supervisor is cultivating authority in his men by providing as many _____ as possible to involve them in tasks affording a challenge. | opportunities

14. Furthermore, the officer should recognize and cite a subordinate when he shows INITIATIVE in the accomplishment of his duties. By commending _____ when it is demonstrated, the supervisor is further motivating the subordinate to excel in his work. | initiative

15. It has been mentioned that the supervisor should commend initiative, but in addition, he should commend his officers for everyday-type GOOD WORK. Too often, a superior criticizes subordinates when they are in the "wrong" but seldom offers praise or encouragement when they steadily produce _____ _____. | good work

16. And finally, the supervisor must remember that if he is to encourage subordinates to utilize AUTHORITY constructively, he must certainly give enough _____ to them to perform the tasks assigned.	authority
17. The leader who is willing to accept _____ from his superiors as an example to his men, who provide his men with _____ to involve themselves in tasks of an advanced nature, who praises _____ as well as _____ _____, and who gives his men the necessary _____ to do their jobs is certainly well on the way then to teaching the constructive use of authority.	responsibility opportunities initiative good work authority
18. And so, to reiterate, a leader should encourage subordinates to use their (a)_____ (c)_____.	authority/ constructively

19. Having reached this point, now list the five ways that you, as a law enforcement or correction officer, can help your men to develop their abilities in the constructive use of authority. (any order) a. _____. b. _____. c. _____. d. _____. e. _____.	Accept responsibility from superiors. Provide challenging opportunities for the men. Praise initiative. Praise good work. Give subordinates the necessary authority to do the job.
20. By so instructing subordinates in the _____ utilization of _____, the leader is preparing his men to face up to, rather than shy away from, the challenge of the job.	constructive authority
21. Having prepared his men in this way, the leader can now confidently DELEGATE some of his assignments to his men. However, in delegating AUTHORITY the leader must realize that he cannot also _____ the RESPONSIBILITY for the ultimate completion of a task assigned to him.	delegate

22. The leader should be aware that ———— always remains with the person to whom the task was originally assigned, even though he may delegate the ———— to do it to one of his subordinates. (This point will be further discussed in Chapter 4, "Leadership and Supervision.")	responsibility authority
23. In concluding our discussion of the first guideline to effective leadership, the law enforcement/correction officer should remember that by teaching subordinates the ———— use of ————, he is not only increasing their worth as officers, but he is also making his job easier by ———— some of his assignments to capable men.	constructive/ authority delegating
24. Attention may now be turned to a second guideline in the development of effective leadership abilities, which is the need to KEEP SUBORDINATES and SUPERIORS INFORMED.	(No response required.)
25. It is essential for the leader to keep both ———— and ———— informed of new developments at all times.	subordinates/ superiors

26. This guideline holds especially true for one's own men. By keeping them ───────, the men will not become confused as to what their functions are, and how well they are doing in fulfilling their part in the overall team effort.	informed
27. Subordinates have a BETTER OUTLOOK, A GOOD UNDERSTANDING OF THEIR ROLES, have a HIGHER MORALE, and FEEL RESPECTED when the time is taken to keep them well briefed.	(No response required.)

28. Therefore, the officer who practices the second guideline to effective leadership, which is to keep ─────── and ─────── ───────, is ensuring that his men have the following:
   a. a better (o)───────.
   b. a good (u)─────── of their ───────.
   c. a higher (m)───────.
   d. a feeling of (r)───────.
	subordinates/ superiors/ informed
	
	outlook
	understanding roles
	morale
	respect

29. In addition to the foregoing, the officer, by assuring that his men are constantly kept ─────── with accurate information, is using the most effective weapon at his disposal to combat rumors.	informed

30. False rumors that are allowed to go unchecked will unquestionably destroy (m)_____.	morale
31. It thus becomes the responsibility of the supervising officer to provide information both verbally and in writing (on bulletin boards, in memos, etc.) to stunt unnecessary friction resulting from a lack of information from (mis)_____.	misinformation
32. As an illustration, let's look for a moment at the correctional facility. If the officers are not aware of the roles of the civilian employees with whom they come into contact, problems may result.	(No response required.)
33. In the above situation, the officer may have frustrated efforts of the civilian staff by enforcing security regulations in a manner which the civilians would interpret as harassment. Had the officers been _____, however, concerning the importance of their civilian counterparts and their unfamiliarity with security procedures, the situation would probably have been handled differently.	informed

34. Therefore, an officer in a supervisory position, has the responsibility of keeping his men _____.	informed
35. Furthermore, a leader must ensure that his men receive information that is CONCISE, CLEAR, COMPLETE AND DISTRIBUTED ADEQUATELY. (You might better remember these four points by their initials—CCCDA.)	(No response required.)
36. Had the uninformed officers in the previous illustration received concise, _____, _____ information concerning the position and importance of the civilian staff, and had this information been distributed _____ throughout the facility, friction between the two staffs might have been avoided.	clear complete adequately

37. CCCDA, then, stands for information that is:
  a. _____.
  b. _____.
  c. _____.
  d. _____ _____.
	
	concise
	clear
	complete
	distributed
	adequately

38. Remember, a *grapevine* doesn't flourish when current, accurate _____ is given to officers on a regular basis.	information
39. One can conclude then that the second leadership guideline—which is that of keeping _____ and _____ _____ — will help to eliminate false rumors which are often causes of discontent.	subordinate superiors/ informed
40. The third leadership guideline, to which we shall now direct our attention, stresses the need to provide ONGOING TRAINING FOR SUBORDINATES.	(No response required.)
41. The plan that the supervisory officer develops in order to provide _____ training for _____ should include FORMAL INSTRUCTION, GROUP DISCUSSION, and ON-THE-JOB TRAINING.	ongoing subordinates
42. The officer, by providing _____ instruction, _____ discussion, and _____-_____-_____ training, will be creating in his men an awareness of their own roles, those of other officers (i.e. crosstraining), and the overall objectives of their unit.	formal group on-the-job

43. Let's look for a moment at the first stage of the training plan—that of _____ instruction. Here there are a number of points to follow if the session is to be successful.	formal
44. First of all, the instructor must KNOW SPECIFICALLY what he PLANS to COVER in the lecture, and he must plan his material according to this estimate. The instructor will undoubtedly present a more purposeful and effective lecture if he _____ _____ what he _____ to _____.	knows specifically plans/cover
45. Secondly, the instructor should be aware of the key elements of his lecture so that they will receive proper EMPHASIS. The instructor will be much more effective in *driving his point home* if he places _____ on the elements of importance.	emphasis
46. Thirdly, the instructor should utilize actual FIELD ILLUSTRATIONS to bring points across in a lively, realistic, and meaningful manner. Thus, it would behoove the instructor to enliven his presentation, whenever possible with the use of _____ _____.	field illustrations

47. Fourthly, the instructor should ENCOURAGE QUESTIONS to ensure understanding. If the men do not learn from the lecture, it becomes a time-wasted affair. The instructor, then, may avoid this waste by _____(ing) _____ from his men.	encouraging questions
48. Fifth and finally, the instructor should REVIEW the MATERIAL discussed at the end of the session. This practice affords the men an opportunity to hear the important points of the lecture again, and thus further ensures that they will remember them. Therefore, the instructor, by _____ the _____ at the end, is enhancing the learning process.	reviewing material

49. Hence, in formulating an effective plan for formal instruction, the instructor should:
  a. know what he _____ to _____
  b. (e)_____ important _____
  c. utilize _____ _____
  d. encourage _____
  e. (r)_____ material
	plans/cover emphasize/ points, etc. field illustrations questions review

50. Now, let's direct our attention to the second stage of the training plan, which is (gr)_____ discussion. To be effective, this stage necessitates the creation of an *accepting* atmosphere so that subordinates do not feel that they will look FOOLISH for asking a question.	group
51. Here, it is important to stress the fact that the individual who doesn't ask questions that may arise in his mind is, indeed, the _____ officer, and not the one who asks a seemingly inappropriate question.	foolish
52. The officer should be made to realize that the only foolish question is the one that goes (un)_____ because he is afraid to ask it.	unanswered
53. Moving on to the third stage of the training plan, you will remember that it is concerned with on-the-_____ training.	job

54. In developing an ____-____-____ training program, the supervising officer should give consideration to the following: a. Give the officer FREEDOM to ACT on his own. b. Provide an EXPERIENCED associate to give assistance when needed. c. FOLLOW-UP to ensure that the officer is learning correct field procedures. d. GRADUALLY REMOVE the officer's DEPENDENCE upon others as he gains confidence and knowledge.	on-the-job (No response required.)
55. The key words, then, in the four elements of a good on-the-job training plan are: a. _____to act. b. _____ assistance. c. (f)_____ d. _____ removal of _____.	freedom experienced follow-up gradual/ dependence
56. Now list the key elements again without referring to prior frames. They are: a. _____. b. _____. c. _____. d. _____.	freedom to act experienced assistance follow-up gradual removal of assistance

57. In short, the complete ongoing training plan, which includes ———— instruction, ———— discussion, and ———— training, is invaluable for the officers serving under you. Without it, subordinates may develop bad practices and learn inappropriate methods.	formal group on-the-job
58. Ongoing training is so essential to law enforcement and correction work that it must never be stopped. If training is always ————, the unit will remain sharp. If it ceases, the men will become ineffective.	ongoing
59. Progressive correction and law enforcement work relies heavily upon the principle of continual training being enacted at all departmental levels.	(No response required.)
60. Now, let's explore the fourth, and final, general leadership guideline which is to KNOW YOURSELF AND YOUR MEN.	(No response required.)

61. The officer who is familiar with his own assets and liabilities usually _____ himself well.	knows
62. The officer who recognizes his own strengths and _____ has a real *plus* in his favor in that he can readily determine the traits that should be stressed and those that need improvement.	weaknesses
63. How, then, might an individual go about acquiring a better understanding of himself? The next several frames will be helpful in answering that question.	(No response required.)
64. By continually taking stock of his POSITIVE and NEGATIVE TRAITS, an individual is certain to become better acquainted with _____.	himself
65. If the individual is honest with himself, he will freely admit to his _____ traits as well as to his positive aspects.	negative

66. Another way to gain more insight into one's own abilities and inabilities of leadership would be through exploring the LIVES OF EFFECTIVE LEADERS AND PUBLIC SERVANTS.	(No response required.)
67. Through a study of other leaders, one can often distinguish parallels and differences between his own basic make-up and that of others to a degree that would not have otherwise been possible.	(No response required.)
68. A study, then, of leaders and public servants of the past and present can often illuminate _____ and _____ in the officer's leadership abilities that he would not have otherwise known.	strengths weaknesses
69. Still another method of gaining more insight into oneself is by ELICITING COMMENTS FROM ASSOCIATES which would aid in the honest appraisal of one's efforts and progress.	(No response required.)

70. Since an individual can seldom look at his own faults in a completely objective manner, it becomes essential that the officer be willing to ask for and accept _____ from _____ concerning his abilities to lead others.	comments/ associates

71. To summarize then, an officer must get acquainted with himself if he is to be an effective leader. And he might get to know himself better by doing the following:
   a. taking _____ of his _____ and _____ _____.
   b. learning about other _____ and dedicated _____ _____.
   c. eliciting _____ from _____.
	stock/positive negative traits leaders public servants comments/ associates

72. We might mention here that knowing one's OWN MEN is probably just as important as knowing oneself. Being familiar with each subordinates abilities, weaknesses and needs will aid the officer in the assignment and improvement of his men.	(No response required.)

73. It follows then that both morale and job accomplishment will be substantially strengthened if the leader makes it a point to _____ his _____.	know men
74. The following frames will illustrate some useful ways in which the law enforcement or correction officer and accelerate his understanding of the men under him.	(No response required.)
75. The officer might, first, take the time and effort to OBSERVE SUBORDINATES IN VARIED SITUATIONS. The officer will certainly gain knowledge of how his men act and react to problems encountered on the job if he _____ them in _____ _____.	observes/ varied situations
76. By _____ subordinates in action, the officer gains some insight into their character (i.e., their drives, frustrations, abilities, and inabilities). These observations should assist him in the assignment of tasks and in determining deficiencies to be corrected.	observing

77. Another way the officer can acquire a better understanding of his men is by MAKING HIMSELF ACCESSIBLE TO THEM. The men will not feel uneasy about seeking aid when necessary if the superior is always _____ to them. | accessible

78. Still another method the officer might use to maximize understanding of his subordinates is to familiarize himself with his men through FREQUENT COMMUNICATIONS with them. | (No response required.)

79. The officer, for example, who often speaks with subordinates about personal feelings and interests, as well as about matters of job importance, is gaining a better understanding of his men through _____ _____. | frequent communications

80. To further promote understanding, the supervisory officer should ensure that his men realize their PROBLEMS WILL BE HEARD and that any NECESSARY ACTION will be taken to alleviate them. | (No response required.)

81. A subordinate will be more willing to bring his problems to his supervisor if he knows they will be ———— and that necessary ———— will be taken.	heard action
82. Therefore, the leader who listens to the problems of his men, and who acts on them when necessary, encourages them to confide in him, thus promoting a better ———— of his men.	understanding

83. Consequently, the officer will achieve a greater understanding of his subordinates if he follows a few basic steps. To summarize, they are:
 	
  a. observing ———— in ————————.
 	
  b. being ———— to his ————.
 	
  c. frequent ———— with his men.
 	
  d. ensuring that ———— will be ———— and necessary ———— be ————.
	subordinates
	varied/
	situations
	accessible/
	men
	communi-
	cation
	problems
	heard/action
	taken

84. If we take into consideration these four points along with the three elements of self-understanding that were discussed previously, the principle of knowing oneself and one's subordinates can then be achieved efficaciously.	(No response required.)

85. Before concluding this chapter, let's review for a moment its essential elements. The next several frames will serve to refresh your memory of the topics discussed.	(No response required.)
86. The first general leadership guideline presented in this chapter states that subordinates should be encouraged to ———— their authority ————.	use constructively
87. To encourage the constructive use of authority, the leader should: a. be willing to accept ———— himself. b. provide as many ———— as possible which involve the men in challenging or advanced work. c. commend ————. d. provide the necessary ———— to get the job done.	responsibility opportunities initiative authority
88. The leader must remember that although he can delegate authority, ———— alone assumes the final ———— for job completion.	he/ responsibility
89. A second general guideline emphasizes the need to keep subordinates and superiors ————.	informed

90. By keeping subordinates ———— at all times, the supervisor is helping to stunt the spread of ———— among his men.	informed rumors
91. The initials CCCDA in reference to information given to one's subordinate stands for what? 　a. ————. 　b. ————. 　c. ————. 　d. ———— ————.	 concise clear complete distributed adequately
92. A third general guideline establishes the need for ———— training within a unit.	ongoing
93. The ongoing training plan contains three forms or types of instruction. They are: 　a. ———— instruction. 　b. ———— discussion. 　c. ———— training.	 formal group on-the-job
94. When engaging in formal instruction the lecturer should remember several points that will make his presentation more effective. They are: 　a. know what he ———— to ————. 　b. ———— important ————. 　c. utilize ———— ————. 　d. encourage ————. 　e. ———— material.	 plans/cover emphasize/ points field illustrations questions review

95. When participating in group discussions, the men should be made to understand that there is no such thing as a ———— question.	foolish

96. The essential elements to remember in conducting on-the-job training classes are:
   a. ———— to act.
   b. ———— assistance
   c. (f)————
   d. ———— removal of ————.
	freedom
	experienced
	follow-up
	gradual/
	dependence

97. A fourth general leadership guideline states that the leader must know ———— and his ————.	himself men

98. Three aids to helping a leader get to know himself better are:
   a. taking stock of his ———— ————
   ———— ————.
   b. studying the lives of ———— ———— and ———— ————.
   c. eliciting ———— from associates.
	positive and negative traits
	other leaders
	public servants
	comments

Guidelines of Leadership

99. Some basic steps for the officer to follow if he wants to gain an understanding of his men are: a. observing subordinates in _____ _____. b. being _____ to _____. c. frequent _____. d. ensuring that _____ are _____ and necessary _____ is _____.	varied situations accessible/them communication problems/heard action/taken
100. And so, the four leadership guidelines which, if followed, should aid the law enforcement/correction officer to become a more efficient leader have now been presented.	(No response required.)
101. Their use, along with the desirable leadership traits presented in the previous section, should make the concept of leadership an easier one to follow and improve upon.	(No response required.)

4 LEADERSHIP AND SUPERVISION

Upon completion of this chapter, the student should be able to perform the following objectives:
1. *Explain the six basic elements of good supervision.*
2. *Explain and practice the procedures for the full implementation and utilization of the elements of supervision and leadership contained herein.*

1. A good leader is one who has CONTROL OF HIS MEN, is able to DELEGATE ASSIGNMENTS, and is ultimately capable of ensuring that those assignments are CARRIED OUT.	(No response required.)
2. One may surmise, then, that the mere delegation of an assignment or task doesn't serve any purpose if it is not ———— ———— effectively.	carried out
3. Additionally, the supervisor will soon realize that his job will go to a large extent unaccomplished if he doesn't gain and maintain ———— of his men.	control

66

4. Thus, the true leader can be represented as one who has _____ of _____ _____, is able to delegate _____ and who follows-up to ensure they are _____ _____.	control his men assignments carried out
5. The question now arises as to how the officer might begin developing the aforementioned talents. A good start will be made through a careful study of the concepts in the present chapter entitled _____ and _____.	leadership supervision
6. ORGANIZATION, the first concept with which the aspiring supervisor should concern himself, can be broadly defined as the division and grouping of related functions, the assigning of personnel, establishing channels of communication, maintaining discipline, and the effective coordination and follow-up of all activities to ensure that they are continually directed to the accomplishment of the mission.	(No response required.)

7. The responsibility for the accomplishment of the objective within the organization assigned to him rests with the ―――――. (supervisor/delegated officer)	supervisor
8. As we mentioned in a preceding chapter, the supervisor may delegate authority, but, in fact, he cannot delegate ―――――.	responsibility
9. The officer may then conclude, at this point, that the primary difference between an effective organization and one that functions only marginally is a good ―――――.	supervisor
10. A well functioning organization is one that adapts and grows, and the INFORMED supervisor must be aware of its dynamic nature. The key to any effective organization, then, is an alert and ――――― supervisor.	informed
11. Moreover, the supervisor must be a part of the (gr)――――― within his organization if he is to properly utilize his authority.	growth

12. To illustrate the need for the supervisor to remain abreast of his organization, he would not have the capability to ELIMINATE non-essential work, reports, etc. if he did not keep himself _____ of organizational changes.	abreast
13. In addition to _____ non-essential work within the organization, the supervisor must be able to recognize SHIFTS IN PRIORITIES from one area (post, offense) to another.	eliminating
14. The supervisor, most certainly, would not be aware of _____ in _____ if he were not *in step* with the dynamics of organizational growth.	shifts priorities
15. Still another area in which the supervisor plays an integral role is that of preventing OVERLAPPING OF AUTHORITY. If he were not closely attuned to the organizational *pulse*, he probably would not be aware that any _____ of authority existed.	overlapping

16. And so, the officer should realize the need for a supervisor to always be _____ of organizational change and growth.	aware
17. We have established that the supervisor in an efficiently functioning organization must continually strive to: A. Eliminate _____ work. B. Recognize _____ in _____ from one area, etc. to another. C. Prevent _____ of responsibility.	non-essential shifts/ priorities overlapping
18. Essentially, in working, within an organization, the supervising officer must also endeavor to eliminate CONFUSION. Actions are hampered and morale is lowered when _____ is allowed to run rampart through an organization.	confusion
19. Also, a most important point to the officer in relation to organization is the difference between LINE and STAFF ORGANIZATION.	(No response required.)
20. In making the distinction between the line and staff organization, one need only remember that the line organization consists of personnel actually performing the daily assignments, and the _____ organization primarily serves a support function.	staff

21. Thus, the tasks are performed by the _____ organization, and the _____ organization serves as a supporting agency to assist the accomplishment of the mission.	line/staff
22. Now, let us direct our attention to another element of supervision requiring mention; the use of the CHAIN OF COMMAND.	(No response required.)
23. This ties in with good organization, since improper use of the _____ of _____ will drastically reduce the overall efficiency of the department.	chain command
24. Each officer must feel that he has _____ (several/only one) supervisor(s) if he is to be sure of his role in the command.	only one
25. If the chain of command is properly followed each individual will be responsible to _____ person.	one
26. To ensure organizational unity, the chain of command must be followed in all but one instance; in time of EMERGENCY!	(No response required.)

27. An emergency constitutes immediate injury to, or loss of life or property, preventing the escape of a felon, and those circumstances causing *major* injury to the name of the department.	(No response required.)
28. Circumstances under which normal day-to-day police operations are performed will not necessarily hold true in times of emergency. Therefore, when an ——————— prevails, the officer may be forced to consult higher authority (bypass his supervisor) or to, in fact, act on his own authority when there is no time to do otherwise.	emergency
29. It stands to reason, then, that when faced with the task of neutralizing a serious threat to life, property, the department, or to prevent the escape of a felon you would: (choose the proper course of action) A. Consult your immediate supervisor or his boss (in the event that your supervisor was indisposed) before initiating any action. B. Employ that amount of force necessary to neutralize the threat, then inform your supervisor of your actions.	B.

30. To reiterate the preceding discussion, we might say that the chain of command should always be followed except in _____ of _____.	time/ emergency
31. An emergency situation may be defined as: A. immediate injury to or loss of _____ or _____. B. action resulting in major injury to the _____. C. the escape of a _____.	life property department felon
32. A third element of supervision is the principle of JOB ANALYSIS. It becomes the job of each supervisor of the techniques used to ensure that current METHODS and OPERATIONS are still needed. In so doing, the supervisor is utilizing the principle of _____ _____.	job analysis
33. Each job assignment or procedure must be examined or reexamined from time to time to determine if current _____ and _____ are still needed.	methods/ operations

34. In analyzing any job there are certain basic steps that must be followed. The job must first be BROKEN DOWN and each detail of the position be listed—to the most minute detail.	(No response required.)
35. Once the job procedure is _____ _____, each element must be EXAMINED and questioned.	broken down

36. In other words, the supervisor must _____ the job to determine the following:
  A. WHY it is done the way it is.
  B. WHEN it is done.
  C. WHERE it is performed.
  D. WHO is supposed to do it.
  E. (specifically) HOW it is done.
	examine

37. Therefore, when analyzing any job, the supervisor must first _____ the position _____ and _____ it in every detail.	break down/examine
38. In the examination process, the supervisor must determine the why-when-where-_____ and _____ of the job assignment or position in question.	who how

39. The detailed elements of any job or procedure are examined by determining the following: A. ———— the job is done the way it is. B. ———— it is done. C. ———— it is performed. D. ———— is supposed to perform it. E. (specifically) ———— it is done.	why when where who how
40. Once the break down and examination have been completed, the assignment or procedure—if it is still necessary—should be RECONSTRUCTED.	(No response required.)
41. There are several actions that may be taken in the reconstruction process. Procedures, for example, that show duplication or overlapping may be SIMPLIFIED or COMBINED.	(No response required.)
42. The simplifying and combining of procedures, then, are elements of the ———— process.	reconstruction

43. In addition, priorities have been known to shift over a period of time. When this becomes evident through job analysis, then a need to rearrange ———— exists in the reconstruction process.	priorities
44. Many ACTIONS that were instituted for a good purpose have often remained a part of a job after the purpose has gone. When this is detected, the unnecessary ———— should be ————.	actions/ eliminated
45. The rearrangement of ———— and the elimination of ———— ———— are both a part of the ———— process.	priorities unnecessary/ actions reconstruction
46. A final part of the reconstruction of a job or procedure is that of ADDING NEW TECHNIQUES. If the job is to be done effectively, ———— ———— are essential to a changing and dynamic organization. As times change, so must the ways of coping with crime and rendering service.	new techniques

47. Now, in reconstructing an assignment or procedure, the officer would: A. ———— and ———— procedures. B. rearrange ————. C. eliminate ———— ————. D. add ———— ————.	simplify/combine priorities unnecessary work new techniques
48. The final step in job analysis is to INSTITUTE the new method after approval has been received and after the subordinates have been briefed on the reason(s) for the change.	(No response required.)
49. The steps to take, then, in analyzing any job are: A. (b)———— ————. B. (e)————. C. (r)————. D. (i)————.	break down examine reconstruct institute
50. Now we shall examine a fourth concept that is of value to the supervisor; CONTROL, alluded to in the beginning of the chapter, is an essential element of good supervision.	(No response required.)
51. Supervision would be extremely difficult or almost impossible without ————.	control

52. Therefore, the supervisor should be aware of the importance of those factors that have to do with: A. the DEGREE OF CONTROL possible (i.e., number of men one can supervise effectively). B. the CONTROL RESPONSIBILITY of each supervisor.	(No response required.)
53. Factors effecting the degree of control possible would be: (select the correct responses) A. the complexity of work being done. B. years of service. C. continuity of staff. D. physical territory involved. E. attitude of subordinates toward assignments. F. length of shift.	A,B,C,D,F
54. Mentally place yourself in a supervisor's position and then select from the following list those items that you would believe to be your control responsibilities: A. provide specific instructions. B. ensure authority is commensurate with task.	A,B,C,D,E

C. be accessible in case of emergency. D. continually observe actions of men. E. inspect on a regular basis and occasionally review men's work on a non-scheduled basis. F. delegate as many duties as possible to subordinates.	
55. The number of men that one can effectively supervise has to do with the _____ of _____ possible.	degree/ control
56. The providing of specific instructions to subordinates is one of the _____ _____ of the supervisor.	control/ responsibilities
57. A fifth element of supervision in EFFICIENT PLANNING. There are basically two types of plans; PROCEDURAL and EMERGENCY-TACTICAL.	(No response required.)
58. The plan that makes up the standing operating procedure (SOP) of the operations manual for an organization is called the _____ plan.	procedural

59. The type of plan having to do with day-to-day activities is the ———— plan.	procedural
60. The plan having to do with special activities (riot control, disaster, etc.) is known as the ———— plan.	emergency/ tactical
61. Let us now examine the steps involved in the preparation of a plan. To begin, one must DEFINE THE OBJECTIVES to be covered by the plan.	(No response required.)
62. No plan can be effective if the objectives for which the plan is intended are not ————.	defined
63. Once the ———— have been defined, the next step to take is to DETERMINE PRIORITIES.	objectives
64. By first establishing the objective(s) to be accomplished by the plan, then the ———— in their order of importance become clear.	priorities
65. Having defined the objectives to be covered by the plan, and having determined the ————, the next step becomes that of GATHERING DATA.	priorities

66. The author(s) of the project must acquire all pertinent information possible pertaining to all phases and operations to be included in the plan. For this reason, the third step in preparing the plan is that of ⎯⎯⎯ ⎯⎯⎯.	gathering data
67. Once the ⎯⎯⎯ has been gathered, the next phase of formulating the plan is to DELINEATE DETAILS, i.e. schedule, division of work, availability of support, etc.	data
68. So, the plan is begun by defining objectives, then priorities are determined, and data is gathered. Next comes the task of describing or delineating the ⎯⎯⎯ of the plan.	details
69. When the above steps have been completed, then it is time to ORGANIZE THE PLAN ON PAPER.	(No response required.)
70. Once the plan has been ⎯⎯⎯ on ⎯⎯⎯ and the roughness has been smoothed out, it should then be SUBMITTED FOR SUGGESTIONS.	organized paper

71. The supervisor should never make the mistake of developing an operations plan without soliciting advice and suggestions from those concerned directly and indirectly in the project. Therefore, the plan should be _____ for _____.	submitted suggestions
72. The final procedure in plan development becomes that of PRESENTING THE PLAN TO SUPERIORS. If a thorough and conscientious job has been performed at each of the previous stages of development, the plan should meet with the approval of the _____.	superiors

73. Let us take a moment, now, to review the steps to be followed in the formulation of a plan of operation.
    A. define _____.
    B. determine _____.
    C. gather _____.
    D. delineate _____.
    E. organize _____ on _____.
    F. submit plans for _____.
    G. present plan to _____.
	objectives
	priorities
	data
	details
	plan/paper
	suggestions
	superiors

74. The preparation of a plan is related to the systematic steps taken when faced with a leadership problem. This area, however, will be pursued further in the next chapter.	(No response required.)
75. Let's now examine a sixth, and final, element of supervision—GOOD JOB RELATIONS among subordinates and between supervisor and the officers under him.	(No response required.)
76. Maintaining good job relations with subordinates, peers, and supervisors is something that requires _____ (much/very little) effort.	much
77. If your answer to the previous frame was "very little," then you are either a very exceptional person, having mastered the art so well that you are not consciously aware of the effort you really make to cultivate good relations, or you have a poor relationship with fellow employees.	(No response required.)
78. The point to be made is that good relations do take a conscientious effort on the part of the supervisor if they are to be maintained. Some primary ways to achieve good job relations will be described in the following frames.	(No response required.)

79. If good relations are to be maintained in the department, WORK MUST BE DIVIDED FAIRLY. One of the quickest ways to spark dissention is to *play favorites* when assigning duties. To prevent this from happening, the supervisor must always divide and assign _____ _____.	work fairly
80. Better relations are found where employees are satisfied and content in the job they are doing. Employees seek RECOGNITION both INDIVIDUALLY and COLLECTIVELY as a group. A good supervisor, then, will not be above giving _____ to an individual for a job well done.	recognition
81. The same supervisor will make a point of commending his departments or unit as a _____ when they demonstrate a real team effort in accomplishing the mission at hand.	group
82. Thus, job relations between subordinates and superiors can be significantly improved upon when _____ is given on an individual and a _____ basis for outstanding achievement.	recognition collective, group

Leadership and Supervision

83. Yet another important ingredient in maintaining good job relations is the provision for EQUAL ADVANCEMENT OPPORTUNITIES. Very little cooperation or efficiency can be expected from an employee who feels that he has no chance of ———.	advancement
84. The intelligent, conscientious officer can be expected to put forth his *all* in nearly every assignment he draws. He does this not only for reason of pride, but also in the hope that he will eventually ——— to a position more demanding of his talents.	advance
85. If the supervisor is to encourage subordinates to utilize their abilities to the maximum in all job assignments, he must provide for ——— ——— opportunities.	job advancement
86. To continue, improved job relations will come about if the superior FOLLOWS-UP ON ALL GRIEVANCES PROMPTLY.	(No response required.)
87. It stands to reason that a subordinate will turn out a better job if he knows that his supervisor is interested enough in him to go the extra step to settle or resolve a ——— that is troubling him.	grievance, problem

88. The subordinate who has no recourse for his problems becomes quickly frustrated. However, if he is reasonably satisfied that his grievance will be heard and _____ promptly, harmony can replace mistrust.	followed-up
89. Finally, the supervisor must NOT AVOID DELEGATING AUTHORITY.	(No response required.)
90. The supervisor who expects a task or tasks to be carried out by subordinates, must realize that they require the _____ to accomplish the assignment(s). Otherwise, the efforts of the subordinates will be frustrated.	authority
91. The above situation often occurs when a supervisor is afraid to release his authority. He must realize, however, that his men interpret such action as a lack of trust in them. To prevent this kind of relationship from forming, the supervisor must not avoid _____ _____.	delegating authority

92. To summarize, we have discussed five elements that will prove beneficial to the supervisor in promoting good job relations within the organization. Complete these elements by writing the missing words in the following blanks: A. divide _____ _____. B. give _____ to each _____ and to the _____ as a _____. C. provide equal _____ for _____. D. _____ all _____ promptly. E. don't avoid _____ _____.	work fairly recognition/ man group/whole opportunity/ advancement follow-up/ grievances delegating authority
93. Before concluding this chapter, let's take a moment to reexamine the six elements of leadership with which we have been working.	(No response required.)
94. The first concept presented with which the supervisor will be concerned is that of (or) _____.	organization
95. The supervising officer has the job of eliminating _____ within the organization.	confusion

96. Those personnel actually performing daily assignments are a part of the _____ organization.	line
97. The support element is known as the _____ organization.	staff
98. It is important that each officer feels that he has only one supervisor. Thus the proper use of the _____ of _____ is another essential element of supervision.	chain command
99. It is the job of the supervisor to ensure that current methods and operations are up to date and still have a need. He may accomplish this task through _____ _____.	job analysis
100. A supervisor can only have a small number of men reporting to him if he is to be effective in fulfilling the responsibilities he owes to his subordinates. So, _____ becomes another element of good supervision.	control
101. Certain procedures must be followed in any operation. These procedures are developed from a plan. Thus, a fifth element of supervision is efficient _____.	planning

102. The final element of supervision calling for such things as a fair division of work, proper recognition, advancement, etc., is that of good _____ _____.	job relations
103. Now list the six basic requirements for good supervision in the following blanks: (any order) A. _____. B. _____. C. _____. D. _____. E. _____. F. _____.	organization chain of command job analysis control efficient planning good job relations
104. With the above six elements in mind, the leader-supervisor can begin to approach his role with some confidence and the realization that he has the tools which will be extremely useful when combined with actual experience.	(No response required.)

5 PROBLEM SOLVING

Upon completion of this chapter, the student should be able to complete the following objectives:
1. Explain the procedures for solving problems that arise at the supervisory level.
2. Implement the problem solving process in resolving difficulties.

1. A leader encounters many difficulties of varied magnitudes. He must tackle the tasks assigned to him while simultaneously trying to minimize numerous factors which can have an ADVERSE EFFECT on his potential and that of his men.	(No response required.)
2. Rumors, fears, and ignorance are examples of factors that often have an _____ _____ on both supervisors and subordinates.	adverse effect
3. In the same vein, hesitancy, anxiety, and dishonesty all lead to (pr)_____ in leadership and have an undesirable effect on the department.	problems

4. Thus far in this text, a number of traits and guidelines have been presented which should help the supervisor in preventing the above factors from growing to the point that they would interfere with leadership and the productive utilization of subordinates.	(No response required.)
5. However, the point now under consideration is what can be done to alleviate a problem if prevention has *not* been successful and the _____ outweigh the leadership assets.	problems
6. To illustrate, therefore, how a leader might approach a problem in order to solve it, the particular problem caused by the presence of RUMORS in the department will be used as an example.	(No response required.)
7. A command's ability to function as a team can be affected very unfavorably by _____, especially by those that are not too far fetched.	rumors

8. Suppose, for example, that rumors were increasing concerning certain new policies and regulations in the department. How would the captain of a precinct deal with this difficulty? (choose one)

    A. He should ignore them for a time, thereby, *feeding* as little attention to them as possible.

    B. Let it be known that the spreading of rumors concerning departmental policies and/or regulations is harmful to the morale of the precinct and will not go unpunished.

    C. Follow a pre-planned procedure so designed to provide him with the necessary steps to take in solving the problem.

C.

---

9. In handling any difficulty, there is a general process through which an individual should go in order to successfully solve what is problematic for him.

(No response required.)

---

10. The first step to take in the problem solving process is to OBSERVE THE PRESENCE OF THE PROBLEM.

(No response required.)

11. Now, in the illustration, the police captain has already taken the first step: he _____ the _____ of the _____ by realizing the existence of the rumors.	observed presence/ problem
12. The next step in the problem solving schema is to determine the PROPORTIONS OF THE PROBLEM in question.	(No response required.)
13. In so doing, the police captain finds that the problem, once a minimal one, is becoming greater because the rumors are being allowed to go unchecked and are, in turn, becoming more outlandish. In other words, the problem has grown out of _____.	proportion
14. Having now determined the _____ to which the _____ has developed, the next course of action for the captain to follow is to OPEN UP POSSIBLE METHODS OF DEALING WITH THE PROBLEM.	proportions problem

15. Therefore, the captain, following the realization that the problem of increasing numbers of rumors, with their debilitating effect on morale, must be curbed, he opens up the following possible ———— of ———— with the problem: (choose carefully the most logical alternative that the captain should follow) 1. Give a talk on the harm caused by believing and/or repeating rumors. 2. Post bulletins dealing with the specific rumors being circulated, to eliminate them. 3. Increase the flow of information and communications within the command.	methods/ dealing 3.
16. Upon studying the three alternatives carefully, the captain decides that method numbers ———— and ———— are really no more than a *band-aid* approach in that they are only treating the current symptoms (rumors).	1 / 2
17. On the other hand, method number ———— strikes at the cause of spreading rumors (lack of accurate information being desseminated), and it is seen as the logical choice.	3

18. Therefore, the spreading of rumors can be most effectively curtailed by countering them with an increased ———— of ———— and ———— within the command.	flow/communication information
19. Upon having arrived at a logical course of action in combatting demoralizing rumors, the captain has, in effect, accomplished the next step in solving the problem, which is SELECTING A PARTICULAR COURSE OF ACTION.	(No response required.)
20. The choice of the third alternative from the other possibilities serves as the selection of a particular ———— of ————.	course/action
21. The final step in the problem solving process provides a need to REVIEW THE EFFECTS OF THE ACTION.	(No response required.)
22. After implementing choice number three by having more meetings with lieutenants and sergeants, ensuring they were passing on information to the men, and instituting a weekly intra-command memo on the bulletin board, the captain took the final step: he ———— the ———— of his ————.	reviewed effects/action

96 *Practical Psychology of Leadership for Criminal Justice Officers*

23. In the above instance, the action taken by the captain hypothetically was a success. The men, now being informed better, did not give credance to ——————— without checking them out with their supervisors, who also were kept abreast of daily occurrences.	rumors
24. However, if the action had failed, and theoretically it is possible, the captain would have started the cycle over again, making sure that he had observed the problem in its entirety before considering a battery of solutions again.	(No response required.)

25. To quickly summarize our discussion of this chapter, please list, in the following blank spaces, the steps that make up the problem solving process:
   A. observe ——————— of ———————.
   B. determine ——————— of the ———————.
   C. open ——————— possible ——————— of ——————— with the ———————.
   D. select a ——————— ——————— of ———————.
   E. review ——————— of ———————.
	presence/ problem
	proportions/ problem
	up/methods dealing/ problem
	particular course action
	effects/action

26. Now that the reader has become somewhat familiar with the format for the effective disposition of problems that often confront the police supervisor, he should gain more proficiency by applying them to the following hypothetical problem in an effort to arrive at a logical solution:

The Problem: A line sergeant is becoming aware that graft is high in a certain, well patrolled area of town. These circumstances indicate dishonesty on the part of the officers responsible for the particular section.	(No response required.)

THE FOLLOWING FRAMES ARE RELATED TO THE ABOVE PROBLEM

27. Having reached the above conclusions, the sergeant has obviously realized the _____ of a _____ which is the first step in reaching a solution.	presence/ problem
28. His next step, then, is to _____ the _____ of the problem.	determine proportions

29. In the next several frames, the reader should finish creating the hypothetical problem as well as reach a solution to the problem. For example, the proportions to which the problem has spread have not been clearly described. The reader should do this in the following blanks: | (No answer provided.)

_____
_____
_____
_____.

30. The next course of action is to _____
_____
_____. | open up possible methods of dealing with the problem.

31. List all possible methods of handling the problem in the following blanks: | (No answer provided.)

_____
_____
_____
_____
_____.

32. The sergeant, having reached this stage should _____. | select a particular course of action.

33. The most logical of the alternatives is _____ . Why? _____ .	(No answer provided.)
34. The final stage in reaching a solution to the problem is _____ .	review the effects of the action
35. What were the results of the chosen course of action? _____ .	(No answer provided.)
36. What should be done if the results prove to be unsuccessful? _____ .	start the cycle over again, making sure the problem is observed in its entirety before considering a battery of solutions again

6 A REVIEW

The frames in this chapter are designed to provide the student with a review of those elements of the text deemed essential to a basic understanding of the psychology of leadership. The student will note that the review material is categorized by the respective chapters from which it was taken. If difficulty is encountered in attempting a response to any of these frames, the student should return to the designated chapter of the text for a re-study of that material before progressing further.

Chapter 1:

1. Effective leadership is of extreme importance to any criminal justice agency. These agencies are created to provide protection correction and render a service to the community, state, and the nation.	(No response required.)
2. It is in the course of providing protection and service to the public that the officer finds himself in a position of _____.	leadership
3. When a riot, for example, flares up in a prison, a _____ officer would be called to the scene to quell the disturbance and restore order.	correction

4. Again, a ———— ———— would most probably be the first to be notified when a city suddenly finds itself in the middle of a civil crisis.	law enforcement officer
5. Therefore, the ability of an officer to demonstrate ———— abilities to a high degree of proficiency is tantamount to the safety and well being of the community.	leadership
6. The reader was informed, in the introductory chapter of this text, of the many ways to approach a definition of leadership.. It should be remembered that after rejecting several possible approaches as being deficient, the ———— approach was adopted.	trait
7. The trait approach, though more complete than the other approaches to leadership, is, itself, somewhat lacking in that the list of traits having something to contribute to leadership development is almost (in) ————.	inexhaustible

Chapter 2:

8. Although not a *golden key* to success in itself, the study of _____ _____ seems to be the most effective way of improving one's leadership potential.	leadership traits
9. Leadership is _____ (more/no more) than a combination of particular traits.	more
10. The ability to direct a group of individuals to accomplish or put forth optimal effort to achieve a goal or goals on a continuing basis is called _____.	leadership
11. The officer who is always punctual, who doesn't make excuses for his mistakes, and who can be continually counted on to get the job done is displaying the leadership quality called _____.	dependability
12. Difficulties in interpersonal relations, perennial tardiness, and a high rate of absenteeism should prompt the supervisor to find out what _____ the officer is having.	problems
13. A good leader is always alert to the early signs shown by a subordinate who is having _____.	problems

14. Yet another quality possessed by the leader is that of being able to logically survey all possible alternatives before making a decision. This trait is known as _____.	judgment
15. Emotions and logic don't mix; therefore, a judgment that is to be wise must be free of _____.	emotion
16. A sound judgment, however, depends upon the presence of still another quality which is acquired through readings and studies in the field and becoming more familiar with subordinates. This quality, upon which sound judgment is dependent is known as _____.	knowledge
17. Knowledge, _____ (is/is no) more than simply knowing the rules and regulations that pertain to the job.	is
18. Another, though rarely demonstrated leadership trait points out the need for new approaches and methods to be tried if progress is to be made in any field. This trait, that many people shy away from out of fear of making mistakes, is called _____.	initiative

19. The leader who hopes to be exceptional must act on his own ———— when circumstances demand it.	initiative
20. Since the peace officer deals with a criminal population on a daily basis, the potential for corruption is great. This element brings us then, to yet another trait of the leader which is ————.	integrity
21. The presence of excessive amount of contraband and the show of favoritism toward certain prisoners in a correctional facility both indicate that ———— has been replaced by dishonesty on the part of certain prison personnel.	integrity, honesty
22. Furthermore, the presence of an *unwritten* policy which forbids the giving of a violation to a particular party points to ———— in a police precinct.	dishonesty
23. A sign of dishonesty, however, is not always obvious. It may only be vaguely noticeable in the types of arrests made or not made. Give an example of a dishonest act that may be difficult to identify. ————————————.	(No answer provided.)

24. Most dishonest law enforcement or correction officers ———— (were/ were not) honest when they joined the force.	were
25. The primary danger to integrity occurs when an officer is tempted to make a seemingly ———— concession to a dishonest interest. For it is here that gross violations of integrity begin.	small
26. A form of respect for other individuals expressed in the way a leader interacts with them on a daily basis is summed-up in the leadership trait known as ————.	tact
27. When it becomes necessary for a superior to correct an officer who has made a mistake, it becomes his job to make the officer in question realize that his behavior was incorrect and possibly irresponsible without alienating him. Here, the ————(ful) superior can do this by concentrating on the ———— of the mistake and how it can be avoided, without degrading the ————.	tactful details officer

28. In effect, the superior should, when following up on a wrongdoing, make it clear to all concerned that he is trying to determine _____ the mistake was made, so that it can be corrected.	why
29. A further leadership trait meriting attention has an obvious value in instances where a department has a biased commander who demonstrates favoritism in his assignments, recommendations for promotions, and punishments. The trait called _____ can be of tremendous value in thwarting such misdeeds.	justice
30. Therefore, the officer who is fair with his subordinates, on guard against prejudice, and who does not bear grudges exemplifies _____.	justice
31. The final leadership trait discussed in the text describes an officer who "carries himself and conducts his daily activities in a manner befitting a defender of justice; to the point where he inspires confidence" as one who has _____.	bearing

Chapter 3:

32. The reader will remember that several _____ to effective leadership were developed as outgrowths of the traits just reviewed.	guidelines
33. A leader is placed in command to utilize the individuals assigned to him, not to do their work for them. Therefore, first guideline teaches the constructive use of _____.	authority
34. There are several methods by which a supervisor can encourage his subordinates to utilize their authority constructively. Among them are the following: A. The supervisor should show *his* willingness to take _____ upon himself from his superiors. B. Provide _____ for subordinates to become involved in tasks of an advanced nature. C. Commend (in) _____, correct _____ tactfully, and give counsel on all matters willingly. D. Provide the _____ necessary to perform the tasks assigned. E. Commend subordinates for their _____ work.	 responsibility opportunities initiative errors, etc. authority good

35. The officer occupying a supervisory role at any echelon is well aware of the resulting confusion and turmoil among subordinates when they are forced to operate in a "vacuum unpenetrated by the vital flow of current, accurate information necessary for them to understand their functions and the overall team mission. It is for this reason that a second leadership guideline establishes the need to keep subordinates as well as superiors _____.	informed
36. Remember, constant, accurate information is the greatest weapon a leader has against _____.	rumors
37. Current information should be provided by the superior both _____ and in _____.	verbally/ writing

38. The reader should remember that an officer in a supervisory position has the responsibility of ensuring that information released to subordinates is: (remember the letters CCCDA)
  A. (c)_____.
  B. (c)_____.
  C. (c)_____.
  D. (d)_____ (a) _____.
	clear
	current
	concise
	distributed
	adequately

A Review

39. Another guideline to effective leadership substantiates the need to provide (on) _____ training.	ongoing

40. Ongoing training consists of the following major categories:
  A. _____ instruction.
  B. _____ discussion.
  C. _____ training.
	classroom
	group
	on the job

41. Several points to remember in preparing a plan of formal instruction are:
  A. Know what you _____ to _____.
  B. Be aware of the _____ points in order to _____ them.
  C. Utilize actual _____ illustrations to being points across in a realistic and meaningful manner.
  D. Encourage _____ to ensure understanding.
  E. _____ material at the close of the session.
	plan/teach
	key, important, etc.
	emphasize
	field
	
	questions
	
	Review

110 *Practical Psychology of Leadership for Criminal Justice Officers*

42. If a group discussion is to be successful, the group leader must encourage _____ from the participants.	questions
43. The group leader should further stress that the only foolish question is the one that was never _____, because the officer was afraid he would appear ignorant for asking it.	asked

44. When conducting an on-the-job training session, the supervising officer should:
  A. Give the officer _____ to act on his own.
  B. Provide an _____ associate for the officer to turn to when he needs assistance.
  C. _____ to ensure that the officer is learning correct field procedures.
  D. Gradually remove the officer's _____ upon others as he gains confidence and knowledge.
	authority
	
	experienced
	
	Follow-up
	
	dependence

45. The final leadership guideline presented in this text stresses the need for the officer in a supervisory position to know _____ and his _____.	himself men

46. The officer may attain a better understanding of himself by performing the following functions:
   A. Continually taking stock of his _____ and _____ traits. | positive/negative
   B. Making a personal study of effective _____ and dedicated public _____. | leaders servants
   C. Eliciting _____ from _____ which will aid him in making an honest appraisal of his efforts and progress. | information/associates

47. The following points, if pursued, will prove to be invaluable to the supervisor in providing him with a better understanding of his men:
   A. Observe subordinates in _____ situations. | varied
   B. Be _____ to one's men, so they will not feel uneasy about seeking aid. | accessible
   C. Ensure that one's men realize their problems will be given a hearing and any subsequent _____ possible will be taken. | action
   D. Familiarize oneself with subordinates through frequent _____. | communication

112 *Practical Psychology of Leadership for Criminal Justice Officers*

Chapter 4:

48. The reader should be well aware that organization is of prime concern to the effective law enforcement/correction leader, and that the primary difference between an effective organization and one that functions only marginally is a good ——————.	supervisor
49. The supervisor must possess a keen awareness of the dynamic growth and change representative of the properly functioning organization for he plays an integral role in: A. —————— non-essential work. B. recognizing —————— in priorities. C. preventing —————— of responsibility.	eliminating shifts overlapping
50. The organization consists of both line and staff functions. The —————— organization is composed of those personnel actually performing the daily assignments, and the —————— organization primarily serves a support function.	line staff
51. The chain of command, essential to any organization dictates that each officer should have —————— supervisor to which he reports directly.	one

52. The chain of command must be followed at all times except in time of ———— when it would be feasible to do so.	emergency
53. Each supervisor must be cognizant of the techniques used to ensure that current methods and operations are still needed. The element of supervision that assists him in this task is known as ———— ————.	job analysis
54. The steps to take in analyzing any job are: A. (b) ———— (d) ————. B. (ex)————. C. (re)————. D. (in)————.	break down examine reconstruct institute
55. Every element of a particular job being analyzed must be examined and questioned once it has been ———— ————.	broken down
56. The simplification or combining of procedures, the rearranging of priorities, the rearranging of priorities, the elimination of unnecessary actions, and the addition of new techniques are accomplished in the ———— stage of the job analysis.	reconstruction

57. The final step in job analysis is to institute the new method after _____ has been secured from superiors, and subordinates have been briefed concerning the _____ for the changes.	approval reasons
58. Control is an element of good supervision without which supervision would be extremely difficult. Therefore, it became necessary for the supervisor to be aware of the _____ of control possible, and his control _____.	degree responsibilities
59. Another element of supervision is that of efficient planning of which there are two types of plans. The first deals with day-to-day activities and is called a _____ plan; while the second has to do with special activities, i.e., riot control, disaster, etc. and is called an _____-_____ plan.	procedural emergency-tactical

60. In the preparation of a plan, a number of steps should be followed:
  A. define _____.
  B. determine _____.
  C. gather _____.
  D. delineate _____.
  E. organize _____ on _____.
  F. submit _____ for _____.
	
	objectives
	priorities
	data
	details
	plan/paper
	plan/suggestions

61. The supervisor who divides work fairly, gives recognition to his men individually and collectively, provides equal opportunity for advancement, follows-up promptly on grievances, and doesn't avoid delegating authority has laid the groundwork for the final element of supervision, which is good _____ _____. | job relations

Chapter 5:

62. As any officer who has filed a supervisory position will attest, he is constantly faced with the task of solving problems of varied magnitudes. The process by which the officer can successfully resolve the problem at hand is as follows:
  A. Observe _____ of _____. | presence/ problem
  B. Determine _____ of problem. | proportions
  C. Consider _____ in dealing with the problem. | alternatives
  D. Select a _____ of _____. | course/action
  E. Review effect of _____. | action

63. The officer should realize that his particular course of action in attempting to solve a problem may not always prove effective. When that is the cause, he should _____ _____.	start the cycle over again, observing the problem in its entirety before reaching another possible solution.
64. With the conclusion of this frame, so concludes this the final chapter. It is not within the scope of this book to guarantee that anyone who reads it will become a good leader; no book can make such a promise. It has been, however, the intent of the authors to provide, in these pages, a number of necessary tools with which to build a sound leadership base. It now becomes the task of the reader to take the basic framework provided herein and to expand upon it as he gains experience in the *dynamic field of leadership.*	(No response required.)

ANSWER SHIELD

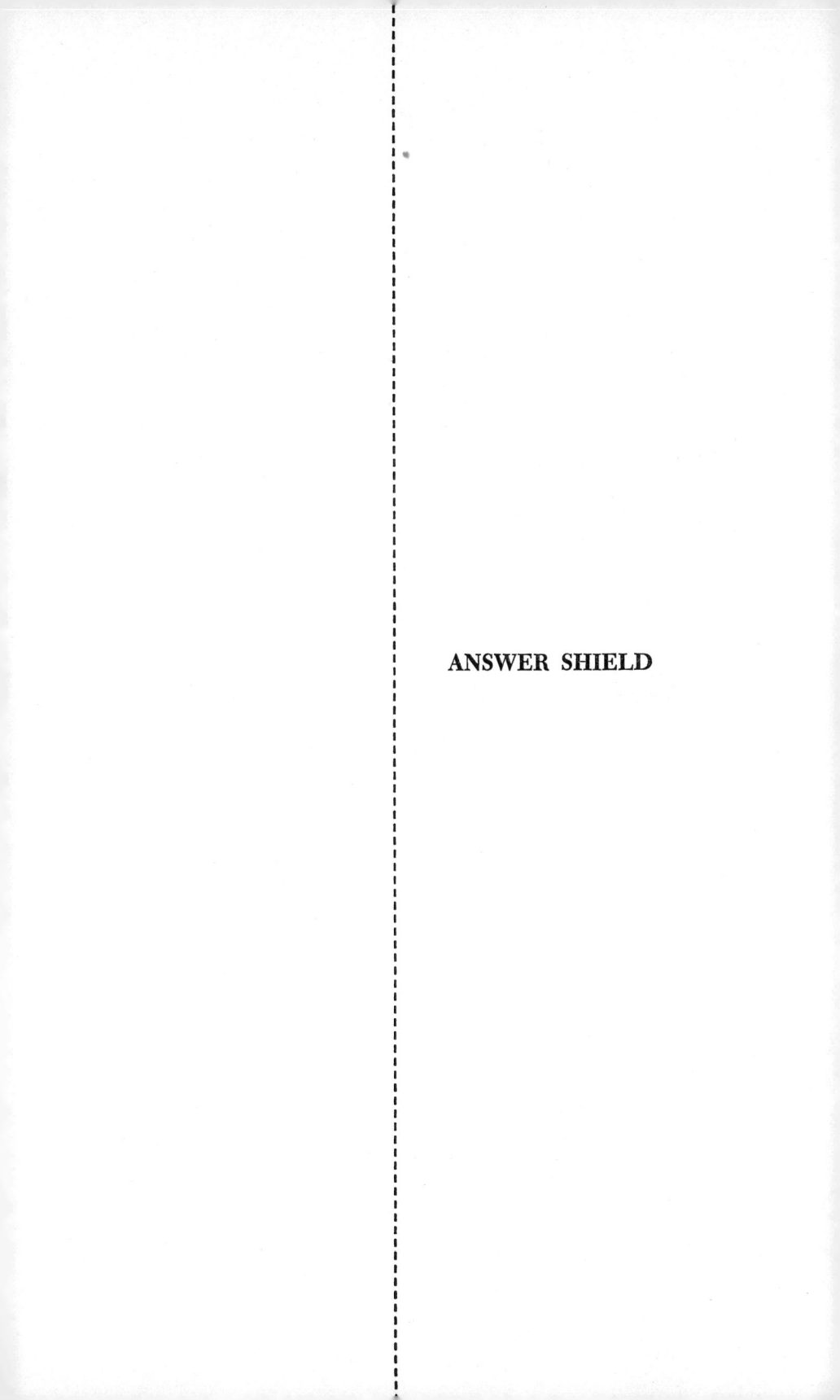